THIS BOOK
BELONGS TO:

My Pregnancy
Record Book

A Treasured Keepsake for a Special Time

A DK PUBLISHING BOOK
www.dk.com

A DK PUBLISHING BOOK
www.dk.com

SP CREATIVE DESIGN
WRITER Heather Thomas
DESIGNER Rolando Ugolini

The team at Dorling Kindersley was:
SENIOR MANAGING ART EDITOR
Lynne Brown
SENIOR MANAGING EDITOR
Corinne Roberts

SENIOR ART EDITOR Karen Ward
SENIOR EDITOR Penny Warren
EDITOR Claire Cross
US EDITOR Iris Rosoff

PRODUCTION Martin Croshaw

First American Edition, 1999
2 4 6 8 10 9 7 5 3 1

Published in the United States by
DK Publishing, Inc.
95 Madison Avenue
New York, New York 10016

Copyright © 1999 Dorling Kindersley
Limited, London

ISBN 0-7894-4122-5

Reproduced in Italy by
GRB Editrice, Verona
Printed and bound in Italy by L.E.G.O.

*I*NTRODUCING THIS BOOK

THIS UNIQUE pregnancy record book is designed in an easily accessible diary format so that you can write down the details of your pregnancy in the spaces provided. Week by week, it adds up to a comprehensive personal record of how your pregnancy is progressing and how you feel at each exciting new stage.

*P*REPARING FOR PREGNANCY

You will find essential information on preconceptual care and preparing for pregnancy so that you and your partner can become as fit as possible for parenthood by changing to a healthier lifestyle.

*H*EALTHY GUIDELINES

At every stage of your pregnancy, there is expert advice on how to stay fit and healthy and how to avoid some of the common complaints that are sometimes associated with pregnancy.

*Y*OUR DEVELOPING BABY

For every month throughout your pregnancy, there is key information on your baby's growth and development. Understanding how your baby develops will help cement the natural bonding process between you and your child.

$\mathcal{G}$ETTING READY FOR BIRTH

There are tips throughout on preparing for labor and the arrival of your baby, including advice on how to draw up your own personal birth plan. Checklists of what to pack for the hospital and shopping lists of baby equipment, clothes, and accessories will help you be fully prepared for the event.

$\mathcal{Y}$OUR PHOTOGRAPHIC RECORD

As well as writing down the intimate details of your pregnancy and birth experience, you can paste in photographs of your newborn baby, making this a lasting and treasured record of one of the most momentous and special times of your life.

$\mathcal{U}$SEFUL INFORMATION

At the back of the book, you will find information on maternity rights and benefits, and the addresses of health support groups.

FEELING CONFIDENT

Being informed about pregnancy will help you be more relaxed and confident during these vital months.

$\mathcal{C}$ONTENTS

PRECONCEPTION DIARY
pages 4 — 11

PREGNANCY DIARY
pages 12 — 47

USEFUL INFORMATION

BEING OVERDUE
pages 48 — 49

WRITING YOUR BIRTH PLAN
pages 50 — 51

MY BIRTH RECORD
pages 52 — 53

PREPARING FOR YOUR BABY
pages 54 — 55

RIGHTS AND BENEFITS
page 56

USEFUL ADDRESSES
page 57

PICTURE GALLERY
(inside back cover)

$\mathscr{P}$LANNING FOR PREGNANCY

HAVING A BABY IS the most natural thing in the world, but there are steps you can take to help make sure your pregnancy is as healthy and happy as possible. The decision to start trying for a baby is probably the most daunting, yet exciting, that you will make. Deciding when the time is right to have a baby is a private and personal decision, to be made by you and your partner.

As more women pursue a career, couples are tending to delay starting a family until they have reached certain stages in their working lives. In fact, a growing number of women are waiting until their mid-thirties and later to have a baby. However, balancing the demands of a successful career with the knowledge that fertility decreases with age can put women under pressure. Also, some couples wait until they feel financially secure before thinking about starting a family. But, remember, you don't have to be a millionaire to give a baby a warm and loving home.

With the decision made, start planning at least three months before you start trying to conceive, so you are in top condition from the moment you become pregnant. If you are using birth control pills, stop taking them now and use a condom while your body settles into its natural rhythm.

Ask your doctor to check your immunity to rubella (German measles). Although a relatively minor illness for adults, rubella can be very damaging to a developing fetus. Even if you know you've been vaccinated, it's worth checking that you are immune.

$\mathcal{F}$OLIC ACID

Now is the time to start taking a daily folic acid supplement. Folic acid is a B vitamin that can help prevent neural tube defects (NTD) such as spina bifida and anencephaly from developing in the fetus. In these conditions, the tissues that form the brain and spinal cord do not develop properly. Women with a previous NTD-affected pregnancy are at higher risk of having another NTD pregnancy. It has recently been found that harelip and cleft palate are also reduced in the babies of mothers who took higher doses of folic acid at the time of conception and in the early part of their pregnancy. It is important that you have an adequate supply of folic acid at the time of conception since the spinal cord is one of the first parts of a fetus to develop.

Folic acid can be found in a variety of foods, including Brussels sprouts, spinach, broccoli, and whole wheat bread. However, it is difficult to obtain the required daily amount of folic acid from food alone. For example, you would need to eat five portions of Brussels sprouts every day to get enough! Folic acid can also be lost when food is stored for a long time or overcooked.

Nutrient needs are much higher during pregnancy. The need for folic acid is more than twice as high. It is important that you be aware of the link between folic acid and neural tube defects. The Department of Health recommends that along with increasing your intake of foods that are high in folic acid, you should also take a 400-microgram supplement every day as soon as you decide you want to become pregnant. If there is a family history of neural tube defects, or if you are epileptic, you will need a higher dose of folic acid, which is available only by prescription. Ask your doctor for advice before trying to conceive. You must take folic acid for the first 12 weeks of your pregnancy as well as before conception to help give your baby the best possible start in life. If you are not sure you are pregnant, the safest course is to take folic acid until pregnancy is ruled out.

THE IMPORTANCE
OF EXERCISE

WHAT SORT OF EXERCISE?

You don't need to belong to an expensive gym to exercise regularly. Instead, you could try some brisk walking or swimming at least three times a week. If you attend an exercise or aerobics class, tell your instructor as soon as you become pregnant, and check that he or she is properly qualified to teach you. You may have to modify your normal exercise program and cut out any aerobics and jerky movements.

However, you should remember that there are certain forms of exercise, such as riding and skiing, that are not recommended for pregnant women. If you are at all unsure, check with your doctor or midwife first.

YOU ARE MORE LIKELY to enjoy your pregnancy if you are relatively fit. This doesn't mean that you have to be an Olympic athlete! If you exercise regularly, you should continue to do so throughout the time you are trying to conceive and once you are pregnant.

My weekly exercise plan

....

....

....

....

....

....

....

....

....

STRETCHING EXERCISES
Gently tilt your head over to one side. Lift your chin and rotate your head to the other side and down. Repeat, starting on the other side. With your head straight, turn it slowly to the left, then back to the middle and then to the right. Repeat.

remember *Relaxation is just as important as exercise for promoting good health and relieving stress.*

PUTTING YOUR FEET UP
Taking time out to relax will bring huge benefits. If you stand for much of the day, relieve tired feet by lying on your back, hugging your knees into your chest.

YOUR PARTNER'S HEALTH

Encourage your partner to get fit and stay fit with you. His level of fitness can affect the quality of his sperm. If your partner is exercising regularly, you both are more likely to stick to a healthy regime. Be aware that a poor diet or too much alcohol can lead to a lower sperm count, so explain to him that what he drinks and eats matters just as much as your diet.

remember *Make sure you tell your exercise instructor when you become pregnant.*

WEIGHT LOSS

Weight-loss diets are not a good idea for pregnant women. They may deprive your body of vital nutrients and could also affect your fertility and general health. If you do want to lose weight, make sure that you go on a diet *before* you start trying to have a baby.

HEALTH TIPS

EVEN BEFORE YOU BECOME pregnant, you can adopt a healthier lifestyle to maximize your chances of having a smooth pregnancy and a healthy baby.

My diet

....

....

....

....

....

....

....

ℋEALTHY NUTRITIONAL FOODS

A balanced diet is essential for keeping you in the best possible shape, and for providing your unborn child with the right start in life. Eat fruits and vegetables raw, or steam them, to preserve a high level of vitamins and minerals.
Make sure you eat a balance of different types of foods—proteins, carbohydrates, and fats. A varied diet of meat, fish, dairy foods, whole grain cereals, fruits, and vegetables will supply everything you need.

WATER OR FRUIT JUICES
Always choose water or unsweetened fruit juices instead of alcoholic drinks. Reduce the amount of alcohol you drink—or, better still, cut it out altogether if you can.

FOLIC ACID
Take a 400-microgram supplement of folic acid every day from the moment you start trying for a baby until you are 12 weeks pregnant.

FOODS TO AVOID

It is advisable to avoid certain foods once you are pregnant. In case you become pregnant sooner than you expect, choose safer alternatives now. Watch out for the following foods:
• Soft, unpasteurized cheeses and liver pâtés because they can cause listeriosis.
• Raw or lightly cooked eggs, which may contain salmonella.
• Liver, because it contains high levels of vitamin A, which can be harmful to an unborn baby.

Problems that result from eating these foods are rare, but they can occur, so it's best to try to avoid them. Make sure that your food is always thoroughly cooked, especially chicken and already prepared meals.

Remember *If you both want to maximize your chances of having a healthy baby, you should give up smoking now. Don't wait until you are pregnant.*

HOUSEHOLD PETS

If you have a cat, then ask someone else to change the litter box, if possible, or wear rubber gloves if you have to do it yourself. Toxoplasmosis, an organism found in cat and dog feces as well as in raw meat, can affect pregnant women, and if the infection is passed on to the unborn child, it can cause serious birth defects.

RELAXATION

Try to take time to relax at this important time in your life. Avoid taking on too much so that you keep your stress level to a minimum.

AVOID STRESS
Make time every day to relax–
just sitting quietly or reading can
reduce tension.

HOW LIFE BEGINS

*F*ERTILIZATION

After each egg is released from the ovary, it is guided into the Fallopian tube, which connects to the uterus (womb). As the egg moves down the Fallopian tube toward the uterus, the womb lining begins to thicken. This is the time in your monthly cycle when you are most fertile—it's the ideal time to have sexual intercourse in order to conceive.

During intercourse, the man releases hundreds of millions of sperm. Some of these will swim up the vagina, through the neck of the uterus—the cervix—into the womb, and on to the Fallopian tubes.

Once in the Fallopian tubes, the sperm may intercept the egg that is traveling down toward the uterus. If the sperm successfully penetrates the egg and fertilizes it, you will become pregnant.

The fertilized egg then travels down the Fallopian tube into the uterus, where it attaches itself firmly to the thickened lining and starts to develop into a fetus. You have created a unique human being.

EVERY WOMAN IS BORN WITH a lifetime supply of eggs, which are stored in the two ovaries. From the onset of puberty—when menstruation begins—these eggs start to be released, usually one each month. This process is called ovulation.

Notes on my menstrual cycle
....
....
....
....
....
....
....

FERTILIZATION OF THE EGG

5 Fertilized egg (zygote)

6 Dividing zygote forms a solid ball of cells.

7 The zygote implants in the uterine wall.

4 Sperm fertilizes the egg.

3 Fimbriae collect the ripe eggs.

1 Ovary produces eggs.

2 Egg follicle releases an egg.

AREA SHOWN IN CROSS SECTION

Boy or Girl?

Each egg contains a single X chromosome, while a sperm may have an X or a Y chromosome. An egg fertilized by an X sperm will create a girl; if fertilized by a Y sperm, it will develop into a baby boy.

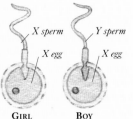

X sperm Y sperm
X egg X egg

GIRL **BOY**

*I*NCREASING THE ODDS

If you are trying for a baby, work out when you are most likely to ovulate. In a regular 28-day menstrual cycle, this will probably be about 12 to 16 days before your next period. Sperm can survive in a woman's body for several days, so the ideal time to have intercourse is the day before you ovulate, because this gives the sperm the maximum possible time to travel into the Fallopian tubes to find the ripe egg.

KNOW YOUR BODY

Every woman's cycle is different, so you need to get to know your own body pattern to work out when you are likely to ovulate. You might find it helpful to use an ovulation-testing kit to find out precisely when you are ovulating. Knowing this could increase your chances of becoming pregnant.

CHANCES OF SUCCESS

No two couples are the same when it comes to having a baby. Some pregnancies happen almost immediately, while others take longer—both are normal. Only half of the couples who are trying for a baby are successful within the first six months. On average, you have a 90 percent chance of getting pregnant within a year.

$\mathcal{N}$OW YOU ARE
PREGNANT

CONGRATULATIONS! Now that your pregnancy has been confirmed, you can embark on an exciting new chapter in your life. This is the special moment for which you and your partner have been waiting. During the next few weeks, your body will start adjusting to being pregnant and you may experience a wide range of unfamiliar and often conflicting feelings. Even though you won't look pregnant yet, the increased hormonal activity in your body may activate sudden mood swings and appetite changes. Don't worry—this is perfectly normal, and you will probably be walking around on cloud nine for days to come.

YOU'RE PREGNANT! Discovering that you are pregnant can be very exciting for both you and your partner.

One of the first decisions that you must make is whom you should tell and when you should do so. This is entirely a matter of personal choice. Obviously, you will tell your partner, and perhaps your immediate family, as soon as you know yourself. However, some women delay telling their friends for a few weeks, usually not until the end of the first trimester (at 12 weeks).

You should tell your employer that you are pregnant when the pregnancy is well established, which will probably be at about three months. You should discuss with your obstetrician or midwife as soon as possible the range of different birth options and prenatal care available. There are many choices to make about labor and delivery and you should be aware of the various options before making up your mind.

YOUR ESTIMATED DATE OF DELIVERY

To work out your due date, find the first day of your last period next to the months in heavy type. The date below is your estimated delivery date.

JANUARY	1 2 3 4 5 6 7 8 9 10 11 12 13 14 15 16 17 18 19 20 21 22 23 24 25 26 27 28 29 30 31
Oct/*Nov*	8 9 10 11 12 13 14 15 16 17 18 19 20 21 22 23 24 25 26 27 28 29 30 31 *1 2 3 4 5 6 7*
FEBRUARY	1 2 3 4 5 6 7 8 9 10 11 12 13 14 15 16 17 18 19 20 21 22 23 24 25 26 27 28
Nov/Dec	*8 9 10 11 12 13 14 15 16 17 18 19 20 21 22 23 24 25 26 27 28 29 30* 1 2 3 4 5
MARCH	1 2 3 4 5 6 7 8 9 10 11 12 13 14 15 16 17 18 19 20 21 22 23 24 25 26 27 28 29 30 31
Dec/*Jan*	6 7 8 9 10 11 12 13 14 15 16 17 18 19 20 21 22 23 24 25 26 27 28 29 30 31 *1 2 3 4 5*
APRIL	1 2 3 4 5 6 7 8 9 10 11 12 13 14 15 16 17 18 19 20 21 22 23 24 25 26 27 28 29 30
Jan/Feb	*6 7 8 9 10 11 12 13 14 15 16 17 18 19 20 21 22 23 24 25 26 27 28 29 30 31* 1 2 3 4
MAY	1 2 3 4 5 6 7 8 9 10 11 12 13 14 15 16 17 18 19 20 21 22 23 24 25 26 27 28 29 30 31
Feb/*Mar*	5 6 7 8 9 10 11 12 13 14 15 16 17 18 19 20 21 22 23 24 25 26 27 28 *1 2 3 4 5 6 7*
JUNE	1 2 3 4 5 6 7 8 9 10 11 12 13 14 15 16 17 18 19 20 21 22 23 24 25 26 27 28 29 30
Mar/Apr	*8 9 10 11 12 13 14 15 16 17 18 19 20 21 22 23 24 25 26 27 28 29 30 31* 1 2 3 5 6 7
JULY	1 2 3 4 5 6 7 8 9 10 11 12 13 14 15 16 17 18 19 20 21 22 23 24 25 26 27 28 29 30 31
Apr/*May*	7 8 9 10 11 12 13 14 15 16 17 18 19 20 21 22 23 24 25 26 27 28 29 30 *1 2 3 4 5 6 7*
AUGUST	1 2 3 4 5 6 7 8 9 10 11 12 13 14 15 16 17 18 19 20 21 22 23 24 25 26 27 28 29 30 31
May/June	*8 9 10 11 12 13 14 15 16 17 18 19 20 21 22 23 24 25 26 27 28 29 30 31* 1 2 3 4 5 6 7
SEPTEMBER	1 2 3 4 5 6 7 8 9 10 11 12 13 14 15 16 17 18 19 20 21 22 23 24 25 26 27 28 29 30
June/*July*	8 9 10 11 12 13 14 15 16 17 18 19 20 21 22 23 24 25 26 27 28 29 30 *1 2 3 4 5 6 7*
OCTOBER	1 2 3 4 5 6 7 8 9 10 11 12 13 14 15 16 17 18 19 20 21 22 23 24 25 26 27 28 29 30 31
July/Aug	*8 9 10 11 12 13 14 15 16 17 18 19 20 21 22 23 24 25 26 27 28 29 30 31* 1 2 3 4 5 6 7
NOVEMBER	1 2 3 4 5 6 7 8 9 10 11 12 13 14 15 16 17 18 19 20 21 22 23 24 25 26 27 28 29 30
Aug/*Sep*	8 9 10 11 12 13 14 15 16 17 18 19 20 21 22 23 24 25 26 27 28 29 30 31 *1 2 3 4 5 6*
DECEMBER	1 2 3 4 5 6 7 8 9 10 11 12 13 14 15 16 17 18 19 20 21 22 23 24 25 26 27 28 29 30 31
Sep/Oct	7 *8 9 10 11 12 13 14 15 16 17 18 19 20 21 22 23 24 25 26 27 28 29 30* 1 2 3 4 5 6 7

ℱERTILIZATION

Fertilization takes place in the Fallopian tube when a sperm penetrates the tough outer membrane of an egg. Once inside the oocyte (the egg's innermost part), the sperm sheds its tail and joins its chromosomes to those of the egg. The fertilized egg cells then divide repeatedly until a blastocyst (a hollow ball of cells) is formed and implants itself in the uterus. At this stage, the pregnancy is established.

A FERTILIZED EGG DIVIDES RAPIDLY

ℐIGNS OF PREGNANCY

- You will miss a period.
- Your breasts will feel heavier and more sensitive.
- The nipple area will deepen in color.
- You may feel very tired.
- You may pass urine more frequently.
- You may feel nauseous, especially early in the morning.
- You may crave certain foods and some foods may taste odd.
- Your sense of smell may be more acute.

○
WEEK 1

Date

My thoughts and feelings

○
WEEK 2

Date

My thoughts and feelings

Remember Don't wait for your pregnancy to be confirmed. Improve your lifestyle now!

USING A PREGNANCY TEST KIT

You can use a pregnancy test kit at home to test a sample of your urine. Most kits work in a similar way to the one shown below. Just hold the absorbent pad of the test wand in your urine stream for a few seconds. Replace the wand in the cartridge and check the results windows after the specified time. For a positive result, both windows will show a color. The absorbent wand reacts if a hormone produced by the embryo is present in your urine.

Results window | Cartridge | Absorbent pad | Test wand

WEEK 3

Date
....

My thoughts and feelings
....

....

....

....

WEEK 4

Date
....

My thoughts and feelings
....

....

....

....

ℰSSENTIAL NUTRIENTS

You provide the food your baby needs to develop and grow, so you must eat a varied, balanced diet. You need:

- PROTEIN Choose chicken, fish, red meat, eggs, lentils, nuts, and dairy products.
- CARBOHYDRATES Opt for unrefined ones, such as whole grain cereals, rice, beans, and pasta. They are all good sources of fiber.
- CALCIUM You need twice as much when pregnant for building the baby's bones and teeth. Eat cheese, milk, yogurt, and green vegetables.
- IRON During pregnancy you need extra iron. Eat lean red meat, spinach, dried apricots, and fish. Increase your intake of vitamin C to aid iron absorption.
- FOLIC ACID Needed for the baby's developing central nervous system. Make sure that you eat plenty of fresh, dark-green vegetables, broccoli, nuts, seeds, and whole wheat bread.

FRESH FRUIT
This is a good source of the vitamins and minerals your baby needs for growth.

WEEK 5

Date

My thoughts and feelings

WEEK 6

Date

My thoughts and feelings

Remember Continue taking your folic acid pills until week twelve.

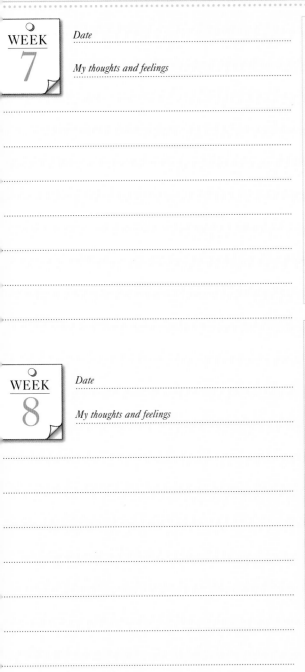

WEEK 7

Date

My thoughts and feelings

WEEK 8

Date

My thoughts and feelings

CONFIRMATION OF PREGNANCY

If your pregnancy has not been confirmed by your obstetrician, schedule a checkup to discuss your pregnancy and the options available to you. Now is the time to find out as much as possible about pregnancy and to ask any questions you may have about your health, labor, and delivery. You may also want to find out about prenatal classes, and you should schedule follow-up appointments.

YOUR BABY

At eight weeks, the fetus is starting to look human, with rudimentary hands and fingers, and feet with toes. The eyes are formed, but the eyelids are still closed over them. Already the basic structure of all the major organs is in place, although the fetus is only about $1\frac{1}{4}$in (3cm) long. The heart has all four chambers and beats about 180 times per minute.

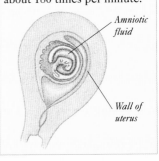

Amniotic fluid

Wall of uterus

$\mathcal{U}$NUSUAL FOOD
CRAVINGS

Rising hormone levels can affect your saliva, making you crave some foods and dislike the taste of others. Don't worry if you suddenly develop a liking for pickled onions. But try to control yearnings for fatty or sugary foods that are high in calories and low in nutrients.

Date

My thoughts and feelings

Date

My thoughts and feelings

$\mathcal{M}$ORNING
SICKNESS

Feeling nauseous is common in early pregnancy, but it usually disappears after the twelfth week. A dry cracker or some toast may help counteract nausea, especially first thing in the morning when your blood sugar levels may be low after a long night's sleep. Avoid eating rich, fried, and spicy food—eat small, bland meals and snacks frequently throughout the day.

WEEK 11

Date

....

My thoughts and feelings

....

....

....

....

....

....

....

....

....

WEEK 12

Date

....

My thoughts and feelings

....

....

....

....

....

....

Remember *Feelings of nausea will soon*

disappear as you enter your

second trimester.

$\mathcal{Y}$OU & YOUR BABY

YOU will now be starting to feel pregnant and, although you will not yet be visibly pregnant to other people, you will probably begin to gain weight as the baby grows rapidly inside you.

YOUR BABY will now look much more human with more clearly defined features. At 12 weeks, he has nearly completed the early phase of his development and can now continue growing. Floating comfortably in a warm sac of amniotic fluid, his bones are developing rapidly and his eyelids are forming. Although he is very active and wriggles a lot, you will not feel his movements yet. He receives vital nourishment via the rich network of blood vessels in the placenta.

BABY IN WOMB

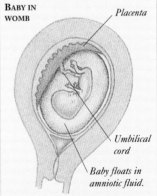

Placenta

Umbilical cord

Baby floats in amniotic fluid.

WEIGHT AND LENGTH
Your baby now weighs about 1.7oz (48g) and is about 2.5in (6cm) long from crown to rump.

WEEK 13

Date
....

My thoughts and feelings
....

....
....
....
....
....
....

*W*ORKING DURING PREGNANCY

You can continue working during your pregnancy. When you stop working depends on how you feel, how far you have to travel, and how stressful your job is. Many women work right up to their due date! Check your work environment to see that there is nothing that could put you or your baby at risk. At work, you should sit down as much as possible.

Remember Tell your employer that you are pregnant and when you plan to stop working.

20

Date
....

My thoughts and feelings
....

....

....

....

....

....

....

....

....

....

YOUR FIRST PRENATAL CHECKUP

You will be asked about your general health, medical history, and pregnancy. You may also be given an internal examination. The following tests will be carried out:

- Measuring your height.
- Noting your weight.
- Testing your urine.
- Testing your blood.
- Monitoring the baby's heartbeat.
- Examining your breasts.
- Checking your blood pressure.

PLANNING YOUR EXERCISE PROGRAM

It's a good idea to plan an exercise program that you can continue throughout your pregnancy. You may have to moderate your exercise regime as you get larger, but even then you can continue with gentle stretching and toning exercises. Regular exercise can help build strength and stamina for labor and maintain muscle tone and flexibility.

THE ANGRY CAT

This exercise eases tired, aching back muscles. Kneel with your arms and legs in line, supporting your weight evenly. Slowly raise your back, dropping your head and shoulders. Breathe out, pulling in your pelvic floor muscles. Inhale slowly and relax.

Keep your hands and knees in line.

*W*HERE THE POUNDS GO

The average weight gain during pregnancy is 28lb (14kg). Mothers who put on this much weight and eat a healthy, nutritious diet tend to have healthy babies and fewer complications. The table below shows how all the extra weight is accounted for:

	pounds
• baby	7½
• enlarged uterus	2
• placenta	1½
• amniotic fluid	2
• enlarged breasts	1½
• increased blood volume	4
• increased body fluid & fat	9½
Total weight gain:	**28**

*E*ATING FOR TWO

Although you are now eating for two, it's quality, not quantity, that counts. To cope with the increased demands of pregnancy, you should eat a highly nutritious diet.
• Eat plenty of fiber-rich foods to avoid constipation and hemorrhoids.
• Avoid the "empty" calories found in cakes, cookies, chocolate, and other desserts.
• Eat plenty of fresh fruits and vegetables every day.
• Enjoy a nutritious snack of low-fat yogurt or fruit.
• Don't eat more just because you are pregnant.

WEEK
15

Date

My thoughts and feelings

Remember You may be eating for two, but you don't have to eat twice as much food!

WEEK

16

Date

....

My thoughts and feelings

....

....

....

....

....

....

....

....

....

YOUR FIRST SCAN

When you have an ultrasound scan, you can see your unborn baby on the screen. It is exciting when you see your baby for the first time. To the untrained eye, a scan may appear blurred, but the technician will help you distinguish the shapes and images on the screen. Scans are done to monitor your baby's progress and check on her health. A routine ultrasound scan will reveal the following:

- The baby's position.
- The baby's growth rate.
- The development of the placenta.
- Whether you are expecting more than one baby.

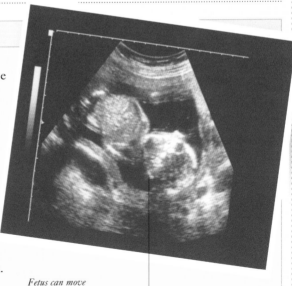

Fetus can move around freely in amniotic fluid.

WEEK 17

Date ....

My thoughts and feelings ....

....

....

....

....

....

....

....

....

....

....

....

SPORTS YOU CAN ENJOY DURING PREGNANCY

Just because you are
pregnant does not mean
that you have to stop
exercising and put your
feet up for nine months.
You can continue to enjoy:

- Swimming
- Walking briskly
- Water aerobics
- Dancing
- Yoga and stretching

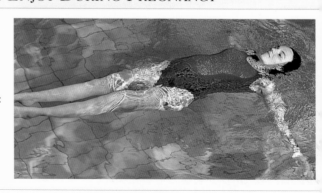

WEEK
18

Date ....

My thoughts and feelings ....

....

....

....

....

....

....

....

....

....

....

....

....

....

....

....

....

Remember To learn more about childbirth and parenting skills, enroll in a prenatal class.

PRENATAL CLASSES

Now is the time to enroll. Classes vary in their ways of teaching so it is a good idea to shop around. Good classes include:

- Practicing relaxation.
- Breathing for labor.
- Practicing positions for labor.
- Rehearsing with your partner.
- Discussing your feelings.
- Learning about breast-feeding.

PREGNANCY HORMONES AND THEIR EFFECTS

During pregnancy, new hormones are produced by your body, and the production of existing hormones increases.

- PROGESTERONE is important for maintaining the pregnancy and relaxing certain muscles in the body.
- ESTROGEN stimulates the development of milk glands and strengthens the womb wall in readiness for labor.
- PROLACTIN helps produce breast milk.
- OXYTOCIN stimulates labor contractions.

CHOOSING A NEW WARDROBE

Date

My thoughts and feelings

By now, your waistline will be expanding and many of your favorite clothes will feel tight. Start thinking about your wardrobe for the coming months. Maternity clothes are loose and comfortable, and flattering to your growing figure. You don't need to buy lots of expensive clothes. Invest in a few standard items that can be worn with loose shirts, T-shirts, sweaters, and jackets.

• **Maternity dress** Loose, flowing dresses are useful for special occasions and could be worn to work too if appropriate.

• **Pants** You can buy fashionable pants or even jeans with an expandable front panel for comfort.

• **Loose tops** Most loosely cut shirts, tunics, jackets, and sweaters can continue to be worn after pregnancy.

• **Skirts and culottes** Like pants, these can be bought with expandable waistbands or stretch front panels.

• **Shoes** Flat or low-heeled shoes are sensible as you get bigger and more unstable.

• **Underwear** You will need a properly fitted, supportive bra with adjustable straps for comfort. Maternity panty hose give good support and are available in many shades.

Remember *You don't have to spend a fortune on maternity clothes— just buy a few classic items.*

WEEK
20

Date
....

My thoughts and feelings
....

....

....

....

....

....

....

....

....

....

....

....

....

YOUR BABY'S MOVEMENTS

At 20 weeks, your baby has developed a nervous system and muscles that allow her to move around inside the womb. She stretches, turns, waves her arms, and swims around in the warm amniotic fluid. It is an amazing experience when you feel her moving inside you for the first time. Initially, your baby's movements will feel like little fluttering butterfly sensations in your stomach, but they will soon get stronger and more noticeable—this is known as "quickening."

YOU & YOUR BABY

YOU are now well into your second trimester and are probably feeling better than ever. Any feelings of nausea should have disappeared, and you are fired up with new energy. Your waistline is disappearing and you may notice the appearance of stretch marks.

YOUR BABY is now well developed, but cannot yet survive outside the uterus because her lungs and digestive system are still immature. She will probably move in response to any pressure that is applied to your abdomen. She can hear the pounding of your pulse, the murmuring of the placenta, and even your voice. Many of her "baby" teeth have formed already, hidden in her gums.

BABY IN WOMB

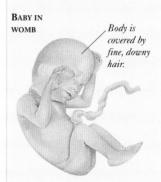

Body is covered by fine, downy hair.

WEIGHT AND LENGTH
Your baby will measure about 7.5in (18.5cm) from crown to rump and weigh around 1lb (0.5kg).

RELAX WITH YOGA

Date

My thoughts and feelings

Practicing yoga on a regular basis throughout pregnancy can promote good health in both you and your unborn child. Yoga exercises are calming, and they help reduce the effects of stress as well as ease aches and pains, especially in your back. Women who do yoga often find that they have easy, shorter labors. If you are already a yoga devotee, continue with your normal exercises, performing them slowly and gently, but stopping right away if you feel any discomfort. If you have not done yoga before, find an experienced instructor who can adapt the exercises to accommodate your enlarging abdomen.

RELAXATION
For total relaxation in yoga, lie on your back with your feet 2ft (60cm) apart, toes turned out, and arms loosely at your sides. Close your eyes and roll your head from side to side. Stretch out your arms and hands, palms upward. Relax your body and stay like this for about 10 minutes.

Remember Relaxation is important—put aside some time to rest every day.

Date
....

My thoughts and feelings
....

....

....

....

....

....

....

....

....

....

....

....

CARING FOR YOUR BABY

You can probably now feel your baby moving inside you. These movements will get stronger as the weeks go by. Already he can taste and smell and hear and respond to noises outside the womb. He can even experience your emotions due to the release of chemicals, such as endorphins, so why not talk to him, play soothing music, and gently touch and rub your abdomen? It will help you get to know and feel close to your baby.

MOVING WELL

Good posture and moving well can help prevent backaches. As you get bigger, your weight can throw you off-balance, causing you to lean backward to compensate and thereby straining your lower back. Instead, when standing, you should lengthen and straighten your back to center the weight of the baby. Drop your shoulders, tuck in your bottom, and lift your chest and ribs. Wear low heels and listen to your body when walking, sitting, or lifting.

LIFTING SOMETHING HEAVY
Bending your knees, crouch down, keeping your back straight. Hold the object close to your body as you lift it up slowly and smoothly.

ＭAKING A BIRTH PLAN

Even though you still have some months to go, you should start thinking about making a birth plan. Write down the sort of birth you would like, with special reference to labor procedures, painkilling drugs, and how you wish to feed your baby. Discuss it with your doctor or midwife to find out what is feasible. For more information on birth plans, turn to page 50.

Date

My thoughts and feelings

AVOIDING VARICOSE VEINS

There is a greater risk of developing varicose veins if you are very overweight or if they run in your family. If you stand for too long, your legs may ache and the veins may bulge as blood pools in the legs. To help avoid varicose veins, follow the guidelines below:

- Wear support stockings.
- Rest with your feet up.
- Don't eat too much salt.
- Do gentle, daily exercise.

PUT YOUR FEET UP
Raise your legs and feet when you are resting.

Place a cushion under your feet for extra comfort.

Date ....

My thoughts and feelings ....

....

....

....

....

....

....

....

....

....

....

....

....

....

....

....

....

Remember **If you suffer from heartburn, eat smaller meals more frequently.**

YOU & YOUR BABY

YOU will now be gaining weight at the rate of about 1lb (0.5kg) per week. Your baby is now beginning to press upward on your stomach and you may get indigestion or heartburn. You should feel your baby moving several times every day.

YOUR BABY is growing slowly but steadily and will soon start to put some weight on her bony frame. Her arms and legs now have their normal amount of muscle. As she gets larger, she takes up more and more of the uterus. Air sacs are forming inside her lungs.

BABY IN WOMB

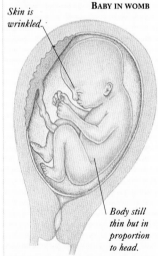

Skin is wrinkled.

Body still thin but in proportion to head.

WEIGHT AND LENGTH
Your baby now weighs just under 2lb (1kg) and measures about 10in (25cm) from crown to rump.

Date

....

My thoughts and feelings

....

....

....

....

....

....

....

Remember Take care of your skin by using fragrant oils and moisturizing creams.

RELAX WITH MASSAGE

A soothing massage can help relieve stress and ease feelings of tiredness. It relaxes aching muscles, particularly in your lower back, and improves your circulation. Massage can be a pleasant experience that you share with your partner.

A SOOTHING TOUCH
If desired, you can use a specially formulated massage oil or a suitable aromatherapy oil to reduce the friction between hands and skin.

LOWER BACK MASSAGE
To relieve a backache, ask your partner to gently massage the lower back and the base of your spine with the heels of the hands.

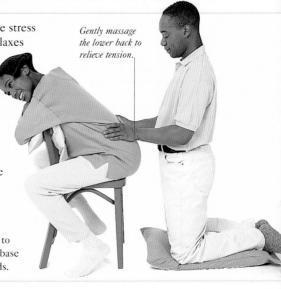

Gently massage the lower back to relieve tension.

Date
....

My thoughts and feelings
....

....
....
....
....
....
....
....
....
....
....
....
....
....
....
....
....
....
....
....
....
....
....
....

Remember Take care to use only massage oils that are safe for pregnant women.

MINIMIZING STRETCH MARKS

Most pregnant women will develop some red stretch marks on their thighs, stomach, or breasts. In time, these should fade to silvery streaks. You can try to avoid them or, at least, minimize them by doing the following:

• Avoid putting on weight too rapidly.
• Eat a healthy, nutritious diet.
• Wear a well-fitting bra to prevent breasts sagging.
• Do regular, gentle exercise.
• Massage with aromatherapy oils containing geranium, mandarin, or neroli.

FEELING BETTER THAN EVER

Now is the time when many women report that they feel better than ever! You may feel really energetic and full of vitality as well as be excited about the new life that is developing inside you. Although your waistline is expanding fast and your pregnancy is now visible for everyone to see, your abdomen is still not large enough to cause discomfort. Hormonal changes mean that your skin may be glowing and radiant, and your hair may be thicker, softer, and glossier than usual. Your friends may comment on how well you look.

YOU & YOUR BABY

YOU are now coming to the end of the second trimester of your pregnancy and you may be starting to feel tired. You will notice the urge to urinate more frequently as the growing baby starts to press on your bladder. As you get larger, sleeping will become more difficult because few positions are comfortable. Try lying on your side with one leg bent, supported by a cushion, and the other stretched out.

YOUR BABY is maturing and continuing to gain weight. As the subcutaneous fat builds up under his skin, he is getting plumper and his wrinkles are disappearing. His eyelids have opened and he can now see and focus inside the uterus – he is aware of darkness and light.

BABY IN WOMB

His hands are fully formed.

WEIGHT AND LENGTH
Your baby weighs about 3lb (1.5kg) and measures around 11in (28cm) from crown to rump.

WEEK 27

Date ....

My thoughts and feelings
....

....

....

....

....

....

....

....

....

....

....

....

....

....

....

....

....

Remember If you are finding it difficult to get to sleep, have a glass of warm milk at bedtime.

34

Date
....

My thoughts and feelings
....

....

....

....

....

....

....

....

....

....

....

....

YOUR BABY'S MOVEMENTS

This is the last month in which your baby will be able to turn a somersault inside the womb. He is now quite large with the proportions of a newborn baby, and there is less space for him to move around freely. Consequently, he will reduce his gymnastics and confine himself to just wriggling and kicking.

HIS POSITION

When your doctor or midwife checks your abdomen, he or she will be able to assess the baby's position. The baby will probably continue lying head upward in the uterus for the coming month, but may turn upside down and "engage" in a head-down position.

EASING HEARTBURN

Now that your abdomen is getting much bigger, you may experience heartburn—an unpleasant burning sensation in your chest just behind the breastbone, sometimes with regurgitation of the stomach acids into the mouth. Heartburn often happens when you lie down, especially when you go to bed at night. Therefore, it is a good idea to sleep with your head and shoulders raised and supported by several pillows. A glass of milk at bedtime may help neutralize acidity in your stomach. Heartburn may also happen when you are lifting heavy weights or coughing. To prevent it, eat light and often; "graze" through the day with smaller meals than usual. Do not eat rich, spicy, or fried foods that may upset your stomach. Stick to simple, nutritious snacks and blander flavors.

PREVENTING HEARTBURN
Avoid large meals and eat small, frequent, nutritious snacks instead throughout the day.

ℬREATHING RHYTHMS

By now you should have joined a prenatal class and been practicing your breathing exercises. Learning to control your breathing can help you relax during labor and ride the contractions, enabling you to push your baby out. Breathe slowly and fully when a contraction starts, then more rapidly as it gets stronger.

𝒟EALING WITH CRAMPS

Cramps are painful contractions of the muscles in the thighs, calves, or feet. They often strike at night and wake you from sleep. They may be caused by a salt deficiency or by low calcium levels in the blood. Ask your doctor.

TAKING ACTION
Massage the affected leg or foot firmly and vigorously. Flex your foot upward toward you, pressing the heel down into the ground. When the pain has eased, walk around to improve the circulation in your feet and legs. For foot cramps, sit with the affected foot and leg stretched out and do circling movements with your lower leg.

Date

My thoughts and feelings

Date

My thoughts and feelings

Remember If you suffer from cramps, tell your doctor — you may need extra calcium, salt, or vitamin D.

MAKE TIME TO RELAX

As you get larger and heavier in the last trimester of your pregnancy, it is more important than ever to make time for relaxation. As well as just resting and taking the weight off your feet, you should also learn the art of positive relaxation to release physical and mental tension.

TENSE AND RELAX

The tense and relax technique is good preparation for labor. Lie on your back, with cushions behind your head. Breathe in and out slowly, focusing on your breathing and clearing anxious thoughts from your mind. Now think about your right hand: tense it and then relax it. Work up the right arm, then the left arm, tensing and relaxing as you go. Then work down your body to your feet. Finally, relax the muscles of your neck and head. You should feel totally relaxed.

GET PLENTY OF REST

As your pregnancy progresses, you may want to take a siesta every day. Just put your feet up or go to bed.

*Y*OU & YOUR BABY

YOU will now have more frequent prenatal checkups to have your blood pressure and urine monitored and the baby's position checked.

YOUR BABY is now perfectly formed, but she is still gaining weight in readiness for birth. Her skin is smooth and pink, she has fingernails, and she may have a lot of hair. Although she is quite well developed, her lungs still need to adjust to respiration outside the womb. If she were born right now, she would probably have difficulty breathing, although her survival chances would be excellent.

BABY IN WOMB

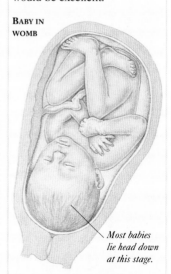

Most babies lie head down at this stage.

WEIGHT AND LENGTH
Your baby weighs about 5lb (2.5kg) and measures around 12in (32cm) from crown to rump.

Date
....

My thoughts and feelings
....
....
....
....
....
....
....
....
....
....
....
....

HOW YOUR BABY IS LYING

Most babies turn head-down in the uterus by 32 weeks and they stay that way until birth. However, a few stay head-up for a little longer, and a minority will remain like this and will be born in a "breech" (bottom-down) position. When your baby has turned head-down, you will feel her feet kicking your ribs, while her head may bounce against your pelvic floor muscles. You may even be able to see your baby moving around at this time by studying the shape of your abdomen and navel.

Date

My thoughts and feelings

member *Even though you are getting heavier, you can continue to keep fit by walking and swimming.*

PLANNING FOR YOUR BABY

ROCK-A-BYE BABY
A crib that you can rock will make a good first bed for your baby.

Now is the time to start preparing for your baby. You can get the nursery ready by doing any necessary decorating and painting, putting up shelves, and fitting a dimmer switch to the overhead lighting system. Start buying some of the baby equipment that you will need—a crib, a car seat, a baby carrier, a carriage or stroller, and a portable baby chair. Shopping for baby clothes and accessories can be fun and will help you bond with your unborn child. To avoid fatigue, do your preparations in short bursts of activity rather than all at once.

PACKING YOUR SUITCASE

This is a good time to get everything ready that you will need, especially if you are going to a hospital. Don't take too many things since there may not be much storage space. All you need are basic night clothes, washing-up things, and comfort aids for labor. Pack your bag now so you won't forget anything in the rush when labor starts.

ESSENTIAL ITEMS
socks
nightgowns
slippers
underwear
bathrobe
sanitary pads
nursing bra
towel and washcloth
breast pads
tissues
hair care items

Date

My thoughts and feelings

Remember Ask your partner to massage your spine gently to ease aches and pains in the lower back.

Date

My thoughts and feelings

$\mathcal{A}$VOIDING BACKACHE

You are more likely to suffer from backache as your pregnancy progresses and the baby's head engages lower in the pelvis. Don't be tempted to lean backward to try to compensate for the extra weight. Instead, you should try to improve your posture and always wear low-heeled shoes.

$\mathcal{F}$EELING HEAVY

When you are feeling heavy, you can get some instant relief by kneeling down and leaning forward with your abdomen supported by a pile of cushions or pillows. This helps take the weight off your back and soothes away any aches and pains. You can also try lying down on your side with your abdomen and the bent knee of your upper leg supported by pillows.

REPARING FOR LABOR
his position may help relieve
e pain of contractions
uring your labor.

$\mathscr{P}$RACTICING YOUR BREATHING FOR LABOR

Practice your breathing now to help you cope with the contractions during labor. Sit cross-legged with your back straight and your hands resting on your abdomen. Breathe in and out slowly, relaxing your abdominal muscles as you breathe out. At the peak of a contraction, breathe quickly in shallow breaths.

$\mathscr{G}$ETTING A GOOD NIGHT'S SLEEP

You need plenty of sleep during the last trimester, but you might find it difficult to get comfortable in bed. A warm bath, a glass of warm milk, and a soothing massage will all help you to relax.

SLEEPING POSITIONS
Never sleep flat on your back in the last weeks—it could restrict the baby's oxygen supply. Instead, lie on your side, supporting your bent leg with pillows.

Date

My thoughts and feelings

COMFORTABLE POSITION
Extra pillows will help support your body.

WEEK 36

Date

....

My thoughts and feelings

....

....

....

....

....

....

....

....

....

....

....

....

....

....

....

....

....

....

....

....

Remember If you haven't already done so, pack your bag for your trip to the hospital.

YOU & YOUR BABY

YOU will now feel very heavy, and will be longing for the birth of your baby. His head should engage in your pelvis very shortly, and this will relieve some discomfort and heaviness. Colostrum—the early protein-rich breast milk —may start leaking from your nipples.

YOUR BABY is almost ready for birth. All he has to do now is put on more fat to help regulate his body temperature after birth. In the womb, he is moving less since he has taken up nearly all the available space. However, you will feel him hiccuping and kicking.

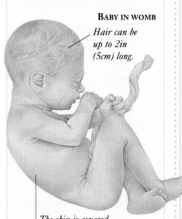

BABY IN WOMB
Hair can be up to 2in (5cm) long.

The skin is covered with vernix.

WEIGHT AND LENGTH
Your baby is now quite plump and weighs about 6lb (3kg). He is nearly 14in (35cm) long from crown to rump.

POSITIONS FOR LABOR

Practice the various positions for labor now so that you can find out which ones are the most comfortable and relaxing. You may want to walk around during the first stage of labor, but as the contractions get stronger, you may need to sit, squat, or kneel.

SITTING FORWARD

Many women find this position comfortable during early labor. Sit facing the back of a chair with your legs straddled on either side. Lean over the chair back, using a pillow to support your head and arms. Rest your head on your folded arms. This position enables you to stay relatively upright.

Head rests on arms.

Lean forward against pillow.

WEEK
37

Date

My thoughts and feelings

Remember Think positively about labor—each contraction is one step closer to your baby.

44

Date

....

My thoughts and feelings

....

....

....

....

....

....

....

....

....

....

....

....

....

APPROACHING BIRTH

The big day when you eventually meet your baby is quickly approaching, and you are probably feeling very impatient and anxious. This is the time when many first-time mothers start to worry about labor and whether they will be able to cope. The prenatal classes should have helped prepare you, along with the breathing exercises and relaxation techniques you have learned and rehearsed. The more relaxed you feel and the fitter and healthier you are, the greater the chances are for an easy, smooth labor and delivery. Don't worry—the months of waiting and preparing for your baby's birth are nearly over.

AROMATHERAPY TO RELAX YOU

Massage with essential plant oils can be very relaxing during your pregnancy. Aromatherapy is a holistic therapy that relaxes the mind and spirit as well as treats the body to promote physical well-being.

However, do be aware that some aromatherapy oils are not recommended for use during your pregnancy. If in doubt, you should always ask a qualified professional for advice. The following oils should always be avoided during pregnancy because they are too astringent: basil, bay, clary, juniper, marjoram, myrrh, pine, sage, and thyme.

OILS YOU CAN USE
Every essential oil has its own distinct fragrance, specific action, and special properties. The essential oils that are recommended in pregnancy include citrus oils, geranium, lavender, neroli, rose, and sandalwood. Never apply just the oil alone—mix 5–10 drops of the essential oil with a carrier oil, such as wheat germ or almond oil. Apply with warm hands directly on the skin and massage gently.

COMFORT AIDS FOR LABOR

There are several items that you can take to the hospital to help you relax and to make your labor and delivery more comfortable. Make sure that you pack in advance. Don't leave this for the last minute when it will get forgotten in the excitement.

CHECKLIST
hot water bottle
small natural sponge
spray water bottle
soothing lip balm
back massager
thick, warm socks
music for relaxation

SIGNS OF LABOR

You may confuse the early contractions in the first stage of labor with the Braxton Hicks contractions that you have experienced.

ONSET OF LABOR
Labor can start in different ways. These include:
• Contractions that resemble a dull backache or strong period pains, becoming more regular with increasing length.
• A "show"—a plug of thick, blood-stained mucus passing out of the vagina.
• Your water breaking—the bag of fluid surrounding the baby ruptures.

WEEK
39

Date

My thoughts and feelings

Date ....

My thoughts and feelings ....

....

....

....

....

....

....

....

....

....

....

....

....

....

....

....

emember *If you're getting really impatient and fed up with waiting, remember, no pregnancy lasts forever and it won't be long now before you meet your baby.*

YOU & YOUR BABY

YOU are now ready for the birth of your child, and your body will be sending you signals that it is preparing for labor. The Braxton Hicks contractions may be more frequent and intense, and you may experience a range of emotions, from anxiety to contentment.

YOUR BABY is now fully mature and fits snugly inside your uterus with little room for movement. Her head has settled deeply into your pelvis, ready for delivery.

BABY IN
WOMB

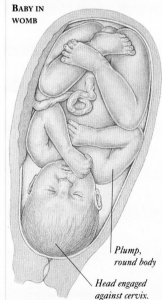

Plump, round body

Head engaged against cervix.

WEIGHT AND LENGTH
Your baby is now about 15in (37cm) from crown to rump and weighs about 6–8lb (3–4kg).

BEING OVERDUE

*D*OES BEING OVERDUE MATTER?

Research has shown that most apparently overdue pregnancies are not late at all—the time of conception has just been calculated incorrectly. However, most doctors still become concerned if the pregnancy continues beyond the forty-second week, and they may well advise inducing.

Most babies grow steadily well into their tenth month in the uterus, but the placenta is now starting to age, and the womb may no longer be the ideal place for the baby. As the placenta becomes less efficient, it may fail to supply adequate oxygen and nutrients to the baby.

An overdue baby who has spent some time in this environment is "post-mature." He may be very thin with dry, peeling skin. He will have longer nails and more hair than other newborn babies.

ONLY A FEW WOMEN GIVE BIRTH on their due date. Most babies are born within two weeks on either side of the estimated delivery date. Don't be disappointed if the big day arrives at last and your baby doesn't! No pregnancy lasts forever, and it is only a matter of days before the waiting is over and your baby is born.

My thoughts and feelings

....

....

....

....

....

....

....

....

....

....

....

Remember *Your doctor will monitor the situation carefully, and will consider the accuracy of your due date and the health of your baby.*

INDUCING LABOR

If you are one or two weeks past your due date and there are signs that your baby is distressed, or your placenta has started to fail, or if you have high blood pressure, you may be induced. This means that the labor is started artificially.

There are three induction methods that hospitals use:
• A pessary is inserted into your vagina.
• Your water is broken.
• You are given a hormone, via an intravenous drip, to make your womb contract.

PRESENTATION FOR LABOR

The way your baby is lying (the presentation) can affect your labor. The most common presentation is with the baby's spine facing outward. However, sometimes the baby's head faces outward, with his spine against yours. Most babies rotate naturally to the correct position before they pass through the birth canal. Some babies present in the breech position and are born feet first.

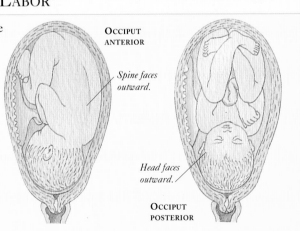

OCCIPUT ANTERIOR

Spine faces outward.

Head faces outward.

OCCIPUT POSTERIOR

$\mathcal{W}$RITING YOUR BIRTH PLAN

A BIRTH PLAN IS A WRITTEN LETTER or list that you make outlining your preferences for the sort of delivery you would like. It should be a comprehensive document, covering everything from pain relief and procedures in labor to contingency plans if problems arise.

WRITING A BIRTH PLAN

THINGS TO CONSIDER	ISSUES
Your birth partner	• Who will be your birth partner: your partner, a friend, or a relative? Can you have more than one person? Do you want your birth partner to leave if you have stitches or a cesarean?
The first stage	• Do you want to be induced if you go past your due date? • Do you want an active labor? • How do you feel about fetal monitoring? • Do you want coaching in breathing and relaxation techniques to relieve the pain in labor? • Do you object to student doctors, midwives, or nurses being present? • Do you want to be offered pain relief? • Do you have preferences for pain relief?
The second stage	• In what position would you prefer to deliver your baby? • Would you prefer to tear naturally or to have an episiotomy? • Would you like to see your baby's head delivered? • Would you like your birth partner to cut the cord? • Would you like your baby placed on your abdomen? • Do you want help with breast-feeding? • Would you and your partner prefer to be left alone with your baby for a short while after the birth?
The third stage	• Would you prefer to deliver the placenta naturally? • How soon would you like to leave the hospital?

Q Who would you like with you at the birth?

Q What is the most important thing to you about your labor?

Q Do you want to be kept informed and share in any decisions made?

Q Are there any things you would like to have in the birth room?

Q What labor procedure do you want?

Q Have you any special requests about the delivery?

Q Do you want the third stage to be speeded up artificially?

Q Do you want to be alone with your baby after the birth?

Q How do you want to feed your baby?

Q Do you want to be awakened at night to feed your baby?

Q What other things are important to you after the birth?

Q Would you like your baby with you or in the nursery?

Y BIRTH RECORD

Date and time of birth
....

Place of birth
....

Who was with me
....

....

Pain relief method
....

Baby's vital statistics–weight, head circumference, length
....

....

....

Apgar score–at 1 minute, at 5 minutes
....

....

Baby's appearance
....

Eyes
....

Hair
....

Looks like
....

....

....

....

My reaction

....

....

....

....

....

Father's reaction

....

....

....

....

....

Other family members' reaction

....

....

....

....

....

....

....

Baby's photograph

𝒫REPARING FOR YOUR BABY

ESSENTIAL BABY CLOTHES	ESSENTIAL BABY ITEMS	SLEEPING AND TRAVEL ITEMS
☐ 1 hat	☐ 2 soft new towels	☐ crib
☐ 6 cotton T-shirts	☐ 8 cloth diapers	☐ baby basket
☐ 2 knitted cardigans	☐ cotton balls	☐ baby carrier
☐ 2 pairs cotton socks	☐ disposable diapers	☐ waterproof mattress
☐ 2 pairs slip-on bootees	☐ diaper cream	☐ cotton sheets
☐ 2 receiving blankets	☐ blunt-edged scissors	☐ light blanket
☐ 6 stretchies	☐ changing mat	☐ colorful mobile
☐ gloves or mittens	☐ baby lotion	☐ intercom
☐ 1 snowsuit	☐ liquid soap	☐ carriage or reclining stroller

☐ cotton nighties, if the stretchie is too hot for your baby during the night

If you use cloth diapers you will also need 2 diaper pails, plastic pants, diaper pins, and liners.

☐ baby car seat, newborn to nine months size

☐ baby sling

☐ portable baby chair

MAKE A LIST
Before you go shopping, make a list of everything you need.

𝒟ON'T WAIT

Don't buy your baby's clothes at the last minute. Go out shopping now while you still feel comfortable enough to enjoy it. Remember that any very small clothes will soon be outgrown, so it's better to buy larger sizes instead.

$\mathcal{N}$OTES

RIGHTS AND BENEFITS

PREGNANT WOMEN ARE ENTITLED to certain rights and benefits. The Family and Medical Leave Act guarantees 12 weeks of "unpaid, job-protected" leave. You may qualify for other benefits under state law and through your employer. If unemployed, you may qualify for government assistance for certain services. Check with local and state health departments for more information.

RIGHTS AND BENEFITS TIMETABLE

WHEN	WHAT YOU NEED TO DO	WHY YOU NEED TO DO IT
BEFORE YOU ARE PREGNANT	Check with your employer to determine the company's maternity leave policies.	To maximize your employee benefits.
AFTER 12 WEEKS	If you are working, inform your employer.	To maximize your employee benefits.
ABOUT 12 WEEKS BEFORE YOUR BABY IS DUE	Discuss your maternity leave plans with your employer.	To negotiate the best maternity leave package possible.
ABOUT 10 WEEKS BEFORE YOUR BABY IS DUE	Give your employer a letter summarizing your maternity leave plans and what you have agreed on.	To clarify your expectations and those of your employer. Gives both of you time to fine-tune plans.
AT LEAST 30 DAYS BEFORE GOING ON MATERNITY LEAVE	Inform your employer in writing.	To protect your rights under the Family and Medical Leave Act.
ONE MONTH MORE OR LESS BEFORE YOUR DUE DATE	Leave work.	To give you time to rest and prepare for the birth.
1–2 DAYS AFTER THE BIRTH	Submit information for birth certificate; apply for Social Security number.	It's easier now than if you wait until later.
2–3 WEEKS AFTER THE BIRTH	Purchase copy of baby's birth certificate	To facilitate record-keeping.

USEFUL ADDRESSES

ACCH (ASSOCIATION FOR THE CARE OF CHILDREN)
10 Woodmont Avenue
Suite 300
Bethesda, MD 20814
Tel: (800) 808-2224
Website: www.acch.org
Premature and high-risk infants

ADOPTIVE FAMILIES OF AMERICA
309 Como Avenue
St. Paul, MN 55108
Tel: (612) 535-4829

AMERICAN ACADEMY OF HUSBAND-COACHED CHILDBIRTH
P.O. Box 5224
Sherman Oaks, CA 91413
Tel: (800) 422-4784

AMERICAN ACADEMY OF PEDIATRICS
141 Northwest Point Blvd.
P. O. Box 927
Elk Grove Village, IL 60007
Tel: (800) 433-9016
Website: www.aap.org

AMERICAN COLLEGE OF NURSE-MIDWIVES
818 Connecticut Avenue NW
Suite 900
Washington, DC 20006
Tel: (888) MIDWIFE
Website: www.midwife.org

AMERICAN RED CROSS
430 17th Street NW
Washington, DC 20006
Tel: (202) 737-8300
Website: www.redcross.org

CESAREAN/SUPPORT EDUCATION AND CONCERN (C/SEC)
22 Forest Road
Framingham, MA 01701
Tel: (508) 877-8266

CHILDHELP USA
Tel: (800) 4-A-CHILD
Parents in crisis, child abuse prevention

DEPRESSION AFTER DELIVERY
P. O. Box 1282
Morrisville, PA 19067
Tel: (800) 944-4773

LA LECHE LEAGUE INTERNATIONAL
1400 Meacham Road
Schaumberg, IL 60173
Tel: (800) LA LECHE
Website: www.lalecheleague.org

MATERNITY CENTER ASSOCIATION
281 Park Avenue South
5th Floor
New York, NY 10010
Tel: (212) 777-5000

MOTHERS AT HOME
8310-A Old Courthouse Road
Vienna, VA 22182
Tel: (703) 827-5903
Website: www.mah.org

NATIONAL ASSOCIATION OF CHILDBEARING CENTERS
3123 Gottschall Road
Perkiomenville, PA 18074
Tel: (215) 234-8068

NATIONAL HEALTH INFORMATION CENTER
P. O. Box 1133
Washington, DC 20013
Tel: (800) 336-4797
Website: www.nhic-nt.health.org

PARENTS WITHOUT PARTNERS
401 North Michigan Avenue
Chicago, IL 60611
Tel: (800) 637-7974
Website: www.parents withoutpartners.org

STEPFAMILY FOUNDATION
333 West End Avenue
New York, NY 10023
Tel: (800) SKY STEP
Website: www.stepfamily.org

$\mathcal{P}$ICTURE GALLERY

My first scan
Date:
....

Leaving hospital   *Date:*
....

First photograph
Date:
....